"Don't die before you read this."

SEND
LITE*
TO
EVERY
FEAR

The Everyday Hero's Litany

*There's Time To Live The Adventure
Intended For You*

PATRICZIA PETRUS

Send Lite* To Every Fear

PATRICZIA PETRUS

© Patriczia Petrus 2006

Published by 1stWorld Publishing
1100 North 4th St. Fairfield, Iowa 52556
tel: 641-209-5000 • fax: 641-209-3001
web: www.1stworldpublishing.com

First Edition

LCCN: 2006937249
SoftCover ISBN: 978-1-59540-890-7
HardCover ISBN: 978-1-59540-891-4
eBook ISBN: 978-1-59540-892-1

SEND
LITE*
TO
EVERY
FEAR

http://www.sendlitetoeveryfear.com/

http://www.lightwhisperer.com/

Note: Additional reference notes and bibliography may be listed on the website, when necessary.

Light is a vehicle for love;

Love is what sustains us.

A précis (like Cliffs Notes) for:

SEND LITE* TO EVERY FEAR

♦ This is a hero's litany for a bewildered world.

♦ *That hero is you.*

♦ It examines the Wisdom of Fear; and reveals the ultimate & brilliant act of will—*residing within each of us*—that matches any fear.

♦ It offers a poetic case study for using light as an elegant tool of transformation with the potential to schedule *a joyous new defining moment* in the history of this planet.

♦ It shapes a practice to be used deliberately to recapture the magnificent life adventure intended for you.

It's what you can do everyday; and when there's nothing left to do.

Finally, it provides a glimpse of a truly **conscious immortality.**

*Webster's unabridged definition of the word Litany reads: "...akin to GR. **Lite, Prayer or Request**". In this book, I've chosen to use the words Lite and Light interchangeably.

CONTENTS

Letter to Fellow Adventurers/Luminaries 15

Acknowledgments. 18
To the *Author of it All* and those who have remembered the Light

Dedication notes. 20
To our heroic, personal and world families

Preface 22
Light is Alive: How to use this book for maximum radiance

Introduction 24
The point is this: *the premise and a promise*

PART ONE

FINDING THE WISDOM OF FEAR:

*Discover the Brilliant, Ultimate Act of Will and
Use it Deliberately to Create the Life Intended for You*

Reminders and The Practice. . . . . 29 - 83

PART TWO

INTENSIFYING THE PRACTICE

Using the Practice to Fulfill your Earth Experience

Expanding your own light 87
Sending Light to others 88
Attending to Pain and the Wisdom of Pain 90
Mental Stuff. 93
A Note Pad 94
First allow yourself to allow 98
"A Blinding Flash of the Obvious" 100
Success. 102
Money 104
'Ethics' + 'Consumerism' 106
Relationship Light Bytes 108
Loving Other People 110
Relationship Outcome. 112
A Light Review of Life. 114
Sick of Sending Light? 116

Events—*real, imaginary, dreamed, televised* 117

TV and movies: *reel or real?* 119

Transform it for you and for the world. 121

The wisdom of anger, violence and even war 125

Love and war in foreign lands: *Bomblets of wisdom* 127

Are you having fun yet? 129

No strings attached or puppets in sight. 131

Gratitude: *the Creator matches and raises the offer* 133

PART THREE

CONSCIOUS IMMORTALITY

About Death and the Seamless Transition

From the finite to the infinite, at last 138

About reincarnation: *Is it really better in Hawaii?* 139

It is simply not good enough to be immortal if. 141

In conclusion: *a Joyous, New 'Defining Moment'* 143

A brief bibliography 144

Dear Adventurers/Luminaries,

SEND LITE TO EVERY FEAR is the outcome of my deep, spiritual search—a search that has made me the somewhat shallow, though happier, person I am today. I am about to offer the same to you.

In 1997/98, I lived in North Carolina on the mountain top known as the Crest of the Blue Ridge. Living there made for a sometimes rough, though majestic climb. This litany of light took its first breaths on the hiking trails near Blowing Rock, NC, around the Moses Cone Manor. I observed much here. For example, Moses Cone backwards says *"Enoch Says Om"*, sort of.

Well, so much for my actual search except to say those were the years of "being stuck" or at best laying a foundation.

In any case, others have written about those kinds of searches and experiences—among them a few actual *near-death experiences* (NDEs) which prove to be illuminating and expansive. Some searches have indeed revealed the Wisdom of the Ages, while others divulge only *near-life experiences* (NLEs) if I may.

In this book, it is my intention to reveal findings that anyone may use to transform his/her near-life experiences into *fulfilling life experiences*. It is about recapturing the life intended for you. *It's an elegant tool for a bewildered world that reveals the wisdom behind fear.* Though it is now several years since I drafted the original manuscript, I feel it is more important than ever to share this. I anticipate that you will agree.

Originally when this work was compiled, we were looking at

headlines about the extreme events in Oklahoma City, Atlanta and Rancho Santa Fe. Who could predict the defining events to come in September, 2001 and continuing today?

The first draft of this book was a single yellow post-it note on which I wrote: *"send lite to every fear"*. I placed it noticeably on a kitchen counter. I looked at it often and practiced the message. It is transforming.

The Practice herein is about transforming the frustrating, and often, explosive patterns of our lifetime(s). It's about finding our way out of the web of immense and confusing diversity towards the unity in it all. It's about creating *a life worth living on earth, a life of nourishing love and inspired adventure that we have only forgotten.*

Love and Light,

Patriczia

REMINDER TO MYSELF (IN BOLD TYPE)
AND FOR THE WORLD TO READ

It is convoluted of me to think I can teach anyone anything. All any of us can do is be the best we can be so that when another is ready to know and glances our way, we are ready. Keep the heartlight on.

On your mark; get set; go. Send lite to every fear.

ACKNOWLEDGMENTS

Enormous thanks to the many that have brought the message of Light.

From the 5000 years of Vedic science with saints such as Patanjali and Shankara; the Essene heritage and writings of John the Apostle; early 20th Century seekers, such as Omraam Mikhaël Aïvanhov; to current illuminations forwarded by Sanaya Roman from Orin; I am personally grateful for the knowledge and comfort. These and others have also affirmed a powerful case for using Light here on earth.

My intention for *Send Lite to Every Fear* was to assemble information *for this time* from personal notes and experience that magnifies this knowing and enables each of us to *consciously restart our personal lives as well as our world.*

Simply, this is more a matter of 'allowing'; and in the allowing we open to the light and the expansion of happiness in our world. God is forever seeking our attention. *Look around.* We just need to heighten our awareness.

The bibliography lists books which affirm the practice of light and have inspired some reminders. This is the short list of what is out there. These will lead you to others. I have been in the fortunate position to access abundant information both directly—*through experience and daily meditation*—and indirectly as a broadcaster through interviews and the media. This pursuit is a passionate one and tends to leave more scholarly ways behind as one looks inward.

Eventually there is the recognition that *no one solely owns the rights to pure knowledge—pure knowledge resides in everyone's soul.* Having said that, extending recognition to the great Beings who have delivered this knowledge is, in itself, a form of sending light. Thank you all who have allowed and are now allowing a pathway for this knowing.

You are scheduling *a new and joyous, defining moment* in the history of our planet.

DEDICATION NOTES

You are the hero. Deal with it.

When I wrote the original manuscript for this book in 1997, I dedicated it to "the Heroes on Earth."

At that time, I intended it to mean *every person who is on this planet* and in particular, everyone who is *waking up* on this planet. You are the heroes.

We are involved in an original and deliberate endeavor on Earth—designed and intended by each of us here and the *Architect of Creation*. You may perceive yourself as that Architect exclusively or as a magnificent co-creator. It's your choice.

After the year 2001, writers and observers wrote and spoke of heroes daily. This was as a result of those outrageous events in New York City, Washington, D.C., and western Pennsylvania and the truly courageous acts that followed— heroic acts which help us redefine the other nearly unspeakable ones.

Yet again, I dedicate this to *all the heroes on earth. You see, simply by choosing to be here, each of you is heroic.* (Am I reminding you of something you've already guessed?)

I lovingly recognize my own enterprising Hirsch family:

> Justin
>
> Meredith
>
> Emily

Josie

Ethan;

My Petrus family; as well as the members of my *Forever Family in Consciousness;*

My forever feline, *ScuppAnanda*, and all other feline/canine/bovine/equine lightwhisperers.

Carry on.

Send lite to every fear.

PREFACE

HOW TO USE THIS BOOK

LIGHT IS ALIVE. Calling Divine Light (lite) to you is the ultimate prayer. It is the ultimate act of your will and your special gift for living on Earth.

Send Lite to Every Fear is a modern litany and a way to recreate your life every day. If I were seeing this book for the first time, I would probably start reading some back pages first. I would want to know where it's going. Please do that. Then I suggest reading the contents of this book from front to back, beginning to end. It's built somewhat like a musical composition. This could take as little as a couple of hours or a week depending on your time and level of attention and interest.

At some point, you will simply flip the book open and be *exactly where you need to be at that moment. Each page offers wholeness and a blessing.*

For starters, here's a roadmap. Part One of the book is arranged with pages of *REMINDERS* that alternate with pages of *THE PRACTICE.* Part Two combines both, reminders and the practice on the same pages. Part Three, *CONSCIOUS IMMORTALITY,* is one of those mysteries wrapped in a riddle bound in a conundrum *with light added.*

The reminders come from poets, mystics, scholars, everyday people and original thought. They inspire you—if I've done my job—to do the practice, which you may wish to personalize as you go along.

Patriczia Petrus

This knowledge of designing our lives deliberately with light has been with us forever. We have only forgotten. *Light is alive* and waiting for you to call. "The Red Sea didn't part until Moses put his toe in," a friend said to me. Light responds immediately; you do need to ask. However, first we need to remember.

Place the book on your dresser, countertop or desk—or download it on your computer and let the transformation begin.

This is what to do everyday...and when there is nothing left to do. In other words, anytime. Feel the fear; send lite to every fear; heal the fear. I still get goose bumps when I read this message.

It's a simple fact that whatever you put your attention on grows stronger. That includes light, *especially light*. Remember that as you begin, *even a tiny bit of progress is progress*.

As often as possible, have the intention that when you heal something for you personally, you heal it for the world. You will be amazed. Watch the news; only now, continue to send lite as you do. Offer up successes in order that they are made ever more beautiful and *"dream ever more beautifully,*[1]*"* as well.

---

[1] Gitta Mallasz, *Talking with Angels* (Einsiedeln, Switzerland: Daimon Verlag, 1988, 1992). This is a theme of her book and for life.

INTRODUCTION

An Important Premise and Promise

It seems to me that the job we agreed to when arriving on Earth was one of:

1.) *Remembering* who we are and what genius tools we bring to the project, and

2.) *Guiding* the development of a planetary design which brings Light and Matter together in a brand new creation. Eventually, it's all a fix for the heart and the realization that *light is a vehicle for love, and that love sustains us.*

The earth project got started then appears to have gotten stuck in chaos and some beauty, as well. We simply forgot the job description as we forgot who we were. Now as we recall, we need to re-form the darker elements that abound by shining light on them.

Lessons. What Lessons?

What lessons are to be learned are found in the *constructing of the design—not about who we are.* As humans with our *refined nervous systems,* we are already luminaries. We are here deliberately to create and to express, then to share the accomplishment with other universal beings and most importantly with the Author of it All, *or God.* Individualized beings throughout the galaxies are watching to see what we courageous adventurers on earth are doing with the vision. Others are waiting for the 'lesson plans' perhaps to utilize and enhance elsewhere.

Patriczia Petrus

In conclusion, the benefit

A great benefit of the journey is that through the use of light, we begin to regain *consciousness of our immortality* and our choices to be *here, there and everywhere* (The Beatles). We only need 'to allow' the magnificence of it all and to know *it is all here to nourish us.*

Whether you accept the idea of a *forever omnipresence or God* is not necessary to your using light in order to change the present circumstances of your daily life. It is only necessary to remember that light is the vehicle for love and it is love that sustains us.

"...there are four million kinds of lives which a soul can gather after that—one gets a chance to be human...", said Swami Brahmananda Saraswati. I am grateful for that reminder, and so much more.

I personally do not want to be in the dark. I choose light.

REMINDER

Sending lite to every fear is the way of the quiet hero.

A quiet hero is one who—in the presence of seeming difficulty or even tragedy—is able to remember the magnificence of his/her own being.

Spontaneously this magnificence is conferred to those present; and the difficulty is lightened and often transformed into joy or bliss. All of this is done simply with light, *lightness of being.*

THAT HERO IS YOU.

Now, invoke Safety, Courage and Strength. Then proceed.

Patriczia Petrus

PART ONE

FINDING THE WISDOM OF FEAR:
Reminders & The Practice

*Discover the Ultimate, Brilliant Act of Will
&Use it Deliberately to Create the
Life Intended for You*

REMINDERS

"*God had no need*
To enter matter
If it were only to get
Out of it."

—Sri Aurobindo

I am here to experience the never-before experienced.
I am here on Earth to unfold
A new wholeness of Spirit-Matter only possible
In an individual physical body. *THIS IS MY DESTINY*

I am here to *be* the Sweetness and to *taste* It.

REMINDERS

Could it be that transformation on Earth is so much the reality and so imminent that it didn't actually matter to a pre-human soul the size, shape or even condition of the body it got. The only thing that mattered was to get a body and get here. And whatever the body, it was meant to enhance the challenge of the adventure.

And, once in that body, it did/does not even matter if spirit remembers its mission early on in infancy or as late as senility—because any damage sustained can be transmuted *Whenever the light comes on!*

◆◆◆◆

Maharishi Mahesh Yogi reminds us that regaining this memory of absolute being creates the physiology of immortality [2].

2 Geoffrey Wells, Ph.D., "Mistake of the Intellect," MIU Video Magazine (Fairfield, IA: Maharishi University of Management, 1987).

REMINDERS

The path is narrow
Yet well lighted, and utterly clear.
Once recognized, it's a
"Blinding flash of the obvious." (Ariel Tomioka)

So obvious that your Mind and Ego balk—but only at first.

Be patient. Once you recognize it,
Keep on keeping on. Act frankly.
You may even wish to act boldly. Remember, *SAFETY FIRST.*

There was a place for fear, originally, to protect the emerging physical body. Then, fear hijacked creation and became controlling.

There's a definite paradoxical attitude required here—one of combined Vigilance & Nonchalance—in order to succeed with the mission.

EXPECT NOTHING AND KNOW THAT ALL THINGS ARE POSSIBLE

EXPECT NOTHING AND KNOW THAT ALL THINGS ARE POSSIBLE.

EXPECT NOTHING AND KNOW THAT ALL THINGS ARE POSSIBLE.

send lite to every fear

REMINDERS

"Know that there is more good at work than evil."

—I Ching

"Find the Good and Celebrate it."

—Betty Shabazz

"Ye are of God, Little Children,
And have overcome them:
Because greater is He that is in you, than he that is in the
world."

—1 John 4:4

B i b i d i—B o b i d i—Boo. (Cinderella, the Disney film)

This is a good one to use when you find yourself *afraid of your own shadow. You see, that is all that there is.* It is all the same stuff; it is all your Self and some of that happens to be your shadowy self. For fun, we deliberately allow ourselves to explore it on Halloween. Is it possible that all the scary stuff at all other times is also deliberate and we just forgot? *Bibidi-Bobidi-BOO.*

THE PRACTICE

INVITE THE LIGHT:

THEN, SEND LIGHT TO EVERY FEAR.

THIS IS THE MOST YOU CAN DO.

IT IS THE ULTIMATE ACT OF FREE WILL ON EARTH.

IT IS THE HERO'S WAY.

IT'S AN EYES-WIDE-OPEN MEDITATION,
It is a conscious act. It is a Daily Act.

Sometimes, it is a moment-to-moment act.

- ◆ Beckon Light
- ◆ Become Light
- ◆ Broadcast Light

And *TRANSFORM THE PATTERNS OF A LIFETIME.*

Here is a true practice to bring more good into your life and to everyone and everything connected to you.

REMINDERS

THE LIGHT:

1.) Creates

2.) Maintains Creation

3.) Destroys Stagnancy in Creation

Look at these ancient Sanskrit words from *The Upanishads*: no need to understand intellectually.

> saha nāv avatu
> saha nau bhunaktu
> saha vīryam karavāvahai
> tejasvi nāv adhītam astu
> mā vidvisāvahai.

Here's the English translation:

> Let us be together.
> Let us eat together.
> Let us be vital together.
> *Let us be radiating truth, the light of life.*
> *Never shall we denounce anyone, never entertain negativity.*

Personally and globally, we've seen where negative thoughts have taken us.

Be mindful; and when you remember, send light to the negative thoughts.

Send lite to every fear.

Patriczia Petrus

REMINDERS

Pope John Paul II gives us this reminder in his book, *Gift and Mystery* .

"St. Thomas Aquinas explains how with the gifts of the Holy Spirit, a person's whole Spiritual being becomes responsive to God's light not only the light of knowledge but also the inspiration of love."

Aquinas also spoke of acquired knowledge and "Infused Knowledge."

This litany of light itself invites the flow of infused, intuitional, or purest knowledge, the light of transformation—a fix for the mind.

Ultimately, it is all a fix for the Heart.

Say: Light of pure knowledge, enter my heart and mind. I become the Light. I recognize and embrace all that I am; all those connected to me and where I am in this moment. I send Light to it All.

"Thank you God for everyone, for everything and for me." [3]

3 This lovely 'thank you' concludes a prayer written by Jim Goure, founder of United Research, Black Mountain, North Carolina.

THE PRACTICE

Everyday, say:

	I
choose one or all	INVOKE
	CALL
	BECKON
	the
choose one or all	PILLAR OF LIGHT
	SUPREME CREATIVE FORCE
	GOD FORCE
	LIMITLESS LOVE, LIGHT, AND TRUTH
	LIGHT OF THE MOTHER
	MOTHER DIVINE
	DIVINE CREATRIX
	LIGHT OF JESUS
	CHRIST CONSCIOUSNESS
	LIGHT OF SHANKARA
	LIGHT OF THE HOLY SPIRIT

REMINDERS

Everything in Creation desires recognition; it wants to be noticed. When you are faced with the fearful elements, call the Light and transform the dark. Also, it is beneficial to call light before engaging in activity—for more auspicious results.

This is your unique ability as a human.

"ESTABLISHED IN BEING (i.e. infused with the Light), *PERFORM ACTION."*

Originally this was spoken in the ancient Sanskrit language and was written:

"YOGUSTHAH KURUKARMANI."

Today, once we are established in being, we might go shopping or:

"YOGUSTHAH, J.CREW, ARMANI."

—*Meredith Hirsch, Fairfield, IA.*

Light creates what we desire—even designer clothes. And, we don't even have to go outside our homes to fulfill these desires. We go, instead, on-line and type in a few keys. The package arrives at our door often the next day.

Along with our desirable on-line activity comes undesirable 'spam'—those unwanted, disruptive messages that are a fact of life. In a click, however, they are deleted.

Patriczia Petrus

MENTAL SPAM

Delete any negative thoughts, what we might call *the mental spam*, as well. Send a light click; and eliminate them. Avoid entertaining negativity. Send light to these thoughts and delete.

REMINDERS

COMING FACE TO FACE WITH YOUR SELF:
Personal accountability to the max

Take a look at your personal talents, gifts, characteristics; then look at your friends, family, surroundings. All is the out picturing of your creative Self. Your incredible ability to affect Creation, to create, is how you are made in the "image and likeness of God." It's all one. It's all the Self. You are face to face with your Self.

EVERYTHING IN YOUR ENVIRONMENT IS YOU AND IT IS ALSO THERE TO NOURISH YOU. That is the experience of oneness, of unity, of God.

I am the artist, the object of my art as well as the appreciator of my art.

Suddenly, you are aware. You recognize. For the first time you see each thing in your environment as being there to sustain you.

The sky, the grass, the sound of the sea, the satiny sheets on the bed, the pashmina-like fur of your cat—it's all there for you. It's all there to comfort you and nourish you. Send light to it all and dream ever more beautiful dreams.

REMINDERS

I am the Physical System that steps-down Divine Light and "heavenizes" all of creation, myself included

Otherwise;

"Let ignorance reproduce itself until it is weary of its own off-spring."

   —*Kahlil Gibran*

It is a choice.

Diversity (*the world*) is never disconnected from Unity (*the Source of Light*). The Source is just out of sight. There is, however, the memory, though faint, that keeps the Universe alive.

It did not happen by chance that the Intellect got absorbed in the objects of the world and ignored the source. *It was a choice.* Maharishi Mahesh Yogi calls this unfortunate yet reversible circumstance the *Mistake of the Intellect.*

The Light destroys all stagnancy in Creation. It pushes Creation forward.

Then, return the new to the Source; consciously, return the Act of Creation to its Author. You do this with a thought or intention or words. It's gratitude.

That's what I can do, everyday and when there is nothing left to do.

THE PRACTICE

OUTER FOLLOWS INNER.

EVERYDAY,

Invoke: *SAFETY* and *PROTECTION* on this day.

Invoke: *LOVE* AND *LIGHT.*
(Then, the manifested forms follow.)

Invoke:

JOY	TRUTH
COMPASSION	HUMOR
TRUE PLACE	PLENTIFUL RESOURCES
FRIENDLINESS	GENEROSITY
HARMONY	HEALTH
AUTHENTICITY	BALANCE
PATIENCE	SERENITY
VITALITY	FLEXIBILITY & OPENNESS
STAMINA	FREEDOM
COURAGE	SINCERITY
PLAYFULNESS	MOJO

Then, through intention, allow the manifested forms to follow. *Leave the definition of the forms to the Author of Creation; after all, He/She is the Grand Designer.*

Be alert to those definitions as they appear in the forms of *Persons, Places, Events* and *Opportunities*. They are prompts for you to take action. Put your toe in the water. Say "yes" more often.

If you feel Doubt, send lite to the Doubt!

SEND LITE TO EVERY FEAR.

REMINDERS

From the ancient Vedic knowledge of *The Upanishads*: *"AHAM BRAHMASMI"*; translated into English from the original Sanskrit: *"I AM THE UNIVERSE."*

I am everything. I am the totality. *No obstacles exist.*

Perhaps these are *only intellectual words* to you for now. At some moment, you will have an *experience beyond words* but one necessarily *"constructed by the intellect."* [4]

And when this experience arises, the bliss will be so great that *the intellect will never again forget it, or its own True Self.*

When you find yourself overwhelmed with life, you can look up at the sky or at the horizon for immediate relief.

Deepak Chopra, M.D. makes a point of this in his book, *Unconditional Life*, noting that the Vedic literature lists 112 ways to transcend or go beyond the chaos of the mind.

---

4 G. Wells, Ph.D., talk, "Mistake of the Intellect". See earlier note.

REMINDERS

Universal Law is impartial.

"See yourself as powerful and you are.

See yourself as powerless and you are."

—Stuart Wilde

The Light serves you and you serve the Light. Divine Light is unbiased and infinitely abundant. Light is open for business everyday, 24 hours a day. It is faster than 911. You are the transformer of Divine Light for use on Earth. You make the call. But, you need to call. You need to have the intention. That is the Ultimate Act of Will.

Otherwise, the mind and the ego would have you continue to re-hash the same ol', same ol'. Call the Light from the Source. Create anew every time, every day.

The following came from the pulpit of the Rev. Nancy Anderson, Church of Religious Science, Encinitas, California:

> It's the baseball World Series:
> First Umpire: "I call 'em as I see 'em."
> Second Umpire: "I call 'em as they are."
> Third Umpire: *"They're nothing until I call 'em".*

THE PRACTICE

INVOKE IN THE HEART; SAY IT THIS WAY:

"I INVOKE SAFETY AND *PROTECTION* ON THIS DAY.

"I INVOKE *JOY, HARMONY, VITALITY, AND FUN* ON THIS DAY.

"I INVOKE THE *FREQUENCY OF LOVE* INTO MY HEART.

"AS I BECOME AND STABILIZE LOVE AND LIGHT, I RADIATE AND SEND LOVE AND LIGHT TO ALL I MEET TODAY."

REMINDERS

One's ability to act as a transformer of light is connected to how much attention/awareness/focus one *spontaneously* brings to the moment. This grows with the practice. Whatever you put your attention on grows stronger.

Each one's individual awareness is weaker or stronger. Be patient. (Invoke Patience). As the mind identifies more and more with the *great light of creativity*, the force grows stronger.

The changes around you begin to become more noticeable, more quickly, and more often.

Meditation deepens and strengthens the connection. Learn Transcendental Meditation™ to cultivate even more silence and focus in the mind. Meditation is not an end in itself; it is a valid means however. It structures Silence. Silence provides an avenue for Divine Light.

I especially like to invoke light after I've meditated and had a latté.

Then, remember to *BREATHE*.

This Litany is definitely Brainwashing. It washes the brain in Light!

THE PRACTICE

Everyday, I consciously send

> Love and Light
>
> to my mind and body;
>
> to each **child**,
>
> <u>by name and location,</u>
>
> for each to use as they wish;
>
> to each **pet**,
>
> <u>by name and location;</u>
>
> to my **home** and **surroundings**;
>
> to my **vehicle**.

I ask for **harmony**, **vitality**, and **fun** in my surroundings.

Sometimes I am in my vehicle, driving, or on a mountain trail, walking, when I am doing this. I am also sending light ahead of me on the road and on the trail to make it safe. (It's helps to jangle a "bear bell" as well. *Safety first.*)

SEND LITE TO EVERY FEAR.

REMINDERS

All of nature is waiting for Light—the Light of Recognition. Each robin and deer; every flower, tree, and rock; every beach and ocean are waiting. All become more alive when you send lite. All become more beautiful and more authentic. So intend to send Light to each elemental as you come upon it. The attention is scintillating for them. The flowers become more beautiful; each tree more stately; each rock more vital and the deer really do dance. All of nature is getting back on track with your attention—your light.

At the same time, nature returns healing to you. The sound of the wind in the trees, water running in a stream, the sound of the ocean, the smell of grass and flowers, the sun and the breeze on your face, these are the primordial elements which serve and transform you. Give them your light; it's money in the bank for you.

Did you ever wonder why some individuals have magnificent plants and gorgeous pets? It's all about attention. It's all about Light. It is your unique ability to *call light, become light and send light*. Then, remember the fertilizer for the geraniums and bring home the Science Diet for your golden retriever.

Read about Findhorn in northern Scotland. This experiment with Light has been going on for decades. See the website, **www.findhorn.org**.

Patriczia Petrus

I have known about Findhorn for more than 25 years and have spent time with some of the founders, including Peter Caddy and David Spangler. They are steeped in Light and recognize the Divinity in all beings with emphasis on all of nature. I really needed a seat belt the first time I met these two together. Literally, I had to grip the underside of the chair on which I sat so I would not rise up. I was seated in the front row of a room in which they were speaking and I felt hugely embarrassed because I was about to lift off. This was many years ago. Today I would let go.

Light is alive and enlivening. It may take some time to get it to the right speed; but when you do, you had better be wearing your seat belt, as well, and *curb your new, unbridled enthusiasm*. It is important to keep your balance—physically, mentally, emotionally, and spiritually.

Send Lite to Every Fear

REMINDERS

REALITY IS A CONTINUUM:

PastPresentFuture—it's all one.

Dr. Bernie Siegel reminds us in essence that,

"...time is just nature's way of keeping everything from happening at once."

Reality is a continuum. It's all one: *PastPresentFuture*. It is all happening at once which is why you are able to send love and light backwards and forwards in time and reap certain harmonious results in Present time.

When you send light backwards in time, for instance, to the memory of a past event, it changes your relationship with that person or situation in the present moment and going forward.

I am getting ahead of myself. There is a life review in your future as you continue to read which will help you *say 'bye, bye' to the baggage holding you back.*

For now, it is enough to consider that reality unfolds sequentially for our enjoyment and the enjoyment of the Prime Mover.

And, when it does seem "to pour", when everything seems to be happening at once, that's when you **Invoke Balance**.

THE PRACTICE

You are able to send light to an event happening:

- ♦ Today
- ♦ Tomorrow
- ♦ Yesterday.

SAY:

I send light to my meeting with (name), (time), (day and date) whether today or in the future.

SAY:

I send light to the past incident at the (*name the event*, e.g. wedding, lunch with…, date with…), (day, e.g. December 12, 1999); *and even an incident as defining as September 11, 2001*, especially such events as they are remembered.

Do this as often as the past memory comes to mind in order to change the relationship in present time especially when the memory is an uncomfortable one involving lovers, family members, work associates or even strangers.

Keep it simple; yet be specific. However, *avoid asking for a specific outcome.*

Allow the Author of Creation to harmonize the situation.

Do, however, look for subtle, present-time changes in yourself and in your relationship with those involved or in some similar future encounters.

THE PRACTICE

FEELINGS AND EMOTIONS

You are able to hold lite on any *concern, worry, self-criticism,* and *shadowy feeling* whenever it arises in the body, including:

fear/anxiety	anger	rejection	Of being:
doubt	shame	embarrassment	criticized
loss/lack	longing	boredom	attacked
loneliness	frustration	sadness	offended
melancholy	fatigue	regret	sabotaged
annoyance	guilt	disappointment	overly vulnerable
nervousness	grief	over-excitement	obsessive
sentimentality	hopelessness	unbridled enthusiasm	pressured
neediness	self-pity	self-importance	
lack of libido	resistance	vengefulness	
dissatisfaction			

variance *(that seeming distance between what you desire and what you believe you can have).*

Omraam Mikhaël Aïvanhov reminds us that *"the light within you varies in accordance with your thoughts and feelings, your hopes, desires and intentions."* [5]

For a more powerful light, keep your thoughts, feelings, hopes, desires and intentions positive and creative; and keep deleting the spam.

---

5 Omraam Mikhaël Aïvanhov, *Light is a living spirit* (Editions Prosveta, 1998). p 62.

THE PRACTICE

CHECK YOUR FEELINGS AND EMOTIONS NOW.

Send lite to every fear or concern, big or small, which may be in the body or mind at this moment.

Just say it, "I send light to this feeling."

If it's important to you, it's important.

Then watch for mental and intuitive prompts such as *"I need some vitamins or an herb,"* especially if there is fatigue or depression involved. If the prompts repeat themselves, then act on the advice.

Often it is the body that simply needs to be balanced for an emotion to be balanced and lifted. Herbs, for instance, simply remind certain organs in the body how to function; they are forms of light. When the body once again starts performing or raises its level of performance, you may put the supplement aside. Its job is done.

Continue to send light as often as the emotion presents itself—every five minutes, every hour, every other day—whatever it takes.

The Bach flower essence, known as Rescue Remedy, is used similarly to Light. It's to be taken every few minutes while distress is occurring. Use light the same way, that is, frequently when the distress occurs. The instructions for using light are about the same as those for Rescue Remedy. There is a difference, however. *Light is always available to you.*

"*This is big.* When you have the intention of offering/returning a good experience to the Author of Creation, you now create the potential for an even better, often astonishing experience to occur."

"This is a practice that exceeds gratitude; it's a practice that enhances life for you and for the world. It is part of our job description; and it will put this creation—we call Earth—back on track."

THE PRACTICE

TRANSFORMING THE SHADOW SIDE/ OFFERING UP THE BRIGHT SIDE

It is important to send light at the moment you notice each concern or negative feeling arising. These can be triggered by the immediate situation or by a thought of an event scheduled to happen later today, tomorrow, or even by the memory of a past event.

You do not need to know what triggered a negative feeling in order to send lite to the feeling and transform it. Just send the lite. You do not need to figure it out.

Take a moment now to check your feelings. Send light to the bothersome ones immediately.

Likewise, you do not need to know what triggered a never-before experienced positive feeling.

JUST SAY "THANKS" FOR THIS GREAT FEELING AND OFFER IT UP TO THE AUTHOR OF CREATION WHEN IT HAPPENS.

Here's an amazing realization. *When you offer up a great experience, it can be transformed into an even more astonishing experience.* **This is big**. There is more about this later.

Briefly, for now, the idea is to:

◆ *send light to negative feelings for transformation;*

◆ *offer up the positive ones to be made ever more beautiful.*

REMINDERS

"Evil is 'good' that is being formed
But is not yet formed."
                    —*Talking with Angels*

What raw materials these darker feeling offer
As do every challenge, set back, or difficult encounter.

I do not seek these out consciously, but I have a tool to transform them and me when they arise.

"When you see a dark shadow...
You may be sure you have the possibility of the corresponding light."
                    —*Sri Aurobindo*

GRACE HAPPENS

THE PRACTICE

The light transforms:

The light <u>re-forms</u> the dark feelings into true, never-before-known versions of:

> Joy
>
> Bliss
>
> Love
>
> Happiness
>
> Compassion
>
> Exhilaration.

Do you get the picture?

We can work with this. We can actually work with these shadowy feelings that keep coming. They keep returning and <u>will</u> keep returning until they are transformed with the love and light you beckon and become. How can that be—those resistant shadowy inventions?

They are returning for the light. They are returning precisely to be re-formed, reshaped. Just send light to the "li'l devils" as they arrive; it may take some coaxing. But each comes around to the mastery of the Light and is transformed. Send lite to every fear.

Then, the shadowing feeling turns into radiance—your radiance.

What a job we took on when we came to earth—the job of building and transforming with light.

REMINDERS

"THE HIGH MEETS THE LOW ALL IN A SINGLE PLAN."

—Sri Aurobindo

The true Human *is just being formed as SPIRIT and MATTER come together:*

SPIRIT

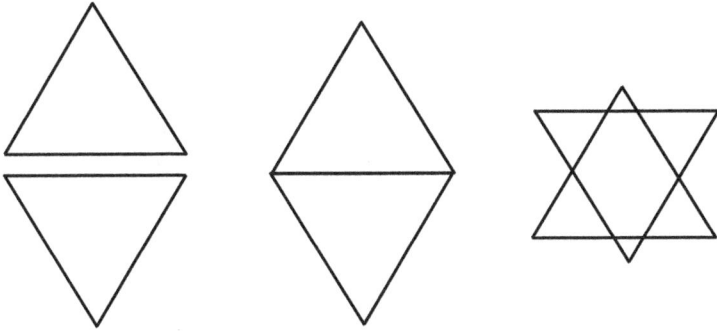

MATTER

...then it appears we become Jewish.

The above supporting illustration was suggested by the book *Talking with Angels* or in this case could have been called *talking with angles.*

REMINDERS

MORE ABOUT THE BOOK, *Talking with Angels*
Budaliget 1943 [6]

A Battlefield for Extreme Enlightenment to Occur

More needs to be said about this remarkable book, *Talking
with Angels*. The title is somewhat contemporary and,
though genuinely applicable, seems almost too *lite* for the
brilliance and intensity of this document translated from
transcriptions made originally in Hungarian.

This book, an incredible documentary published in
Switzerland after World War II, is the actual account of a
group of four, thirty- something artistic Hungarians in hid-
ing, who were open to receiving special spiritual information
while simultaneously being spectators to the war on a day-
to-day basis. This work truly defines the term *co-existence of
opposites* and the circumstances provide a stage for *extreme
enlightenment*, i.e., being in a most challenging, life-and-
death situation in order for the divine light to enter. More on
this later.

The translation did speak of Angels, specifically as:

> *Angels of Build*
> *Angels of Measure*
> *Angels of Help &*
> *Angels of Shine.*

At the time, all were available to the Hungarians and are still available to us today. Give these angels a call. As do many other humans, I have an invaluable relationship with Angels, who personalize the Light for me when I require that. Send lite to every fear.

6 This is the complete name of the later edition. All references, herein, however, were taken from the earlier editions. See notes and bibliography.

REMINDERS

DIVINE CIRCULATION

I *ASK* for the Light:

I *RECEIVE* the Light;

The difficulty if dissolved.

I consciously *OFFER* the resulting good to the Author of Creation,

Who *RETURNS* greater good to me on earth.

The bold becomes bolder;

The beautiful becomes more beautiful;

Turbulent emotions become more refined eventually disappearing into an ocean of bliss.

Is this Heaven on Earth or what! It could be. *YOU CARRY THE SEEDS*.

No need to fake this one. Eventually all strong emotions transform in the presence of the Light. That's when to say "Thanks", when you are actually feeling better. Then, offer it up on the wave of that feeling.

Until you feel the change, keep sending lite to the fear or emotion or concern and go about your business.

REMINDERS

The Wisdom behind Fear

Are you beginning to see the wisdom of fear and other strong emotions such as anger and jealousy yet? The wisdom is that these emotions carry the seeds of love. When transformed by light, they bring more love to our world. Eventually they bring a total experience of Unity, that we all are One. Through the alchemy of your attention and light, they open the door to It All.

All actions are either Fear-Based or Love-Based.

Check in with yourself when you are considering an action. Are you acting out of Fear (fear of losing someone or something) or out of Love (intending happiness for all concerned)?

This is important: when you are unsure, avoid self-criticism. Be 100 percent compassionate with yourself at all times, about everything. This is tantamount to loving yourself first. Remember to nurture yourself in order to serve others.

Then, simply, have the intent of acting out of love towards other.

That's the most you can ever do.

"Say it.

Think it.

Feel it.

'I offer my joy to the Author of Creation. I offer this most beautiful moment.'

This completes the circle. You have called the Light and utilized the Light and are ready to return a worthy result to the Creator."

THE PRACTICE

THE COMPLETE AND ULTIMATE ACT OF WILL

When your feelings lighten up, that is the time to ride the wave and say Thanks.

Then, OFFER UP THE EXPERIENCE...

Say: "I offer up this:

        Lightness of Being

        Joy

        Happiness

        Vitality

        Exhilaration

        Security and Well Being."

Consciously express gratitude as you offer the newly-formed feeling to the Author, the Creator.

Say it, think it, feel it: "I offer my joy to the Author of Creation. I offer this most beautiful moment."

Consciously calling the Light and returning the result is the complete and ultimate act of will.

REMINDERS

The recognition of Beauty is the recognition of the Divine in the world.

This delights the Creator and allows for greater, better, more refined experiences to come back to you and the world.

The point here is that this is not a gratitude that simply guarantees more of the same; *this recognition holds the promise of an even more beautiful, expansive and refined experience coming back to you and the world. You are offering a beautiful work of art to be made even more beautiful.*

This is the difference. This is putting creation in the direction intended in the first place.

Patriczia Petrus

REMINDERS

"The affectionate dedication of the human will to the Father's will is man's choicest gift to God: In fact, such a creation of creative will constitute man's only possible gift of true value to the Paradise Father."

—The Urantia Book

We've all heard this before in some way. The question has been "why would I want to do this?" Well, when you've had enough difficult relationships, endless frustrations and shake-ups in your own home and life or have watched others suffering on your television screen, this is all that is left to do. Then the next question is how. This hero's litany guides you across bumpy water to discover a new, halcyon harbor.

REMINDERS

FACE/OFF!

See it all as the Self—the good and the evil, the Angel and the Dragon.

This may be why—because it is all the Self—that the lead actors in the 1997 film *Face/Off* so easily play both the good and evil characters. The unique plot requires the actors to each play two personalities—hero and villain. *Isn't that actually a choice each of us makes daily?*

And why is it that many actors say playing evil is more fun? This may be then the reason 'evil' continues on earth—because it is interesting and makes us feel 'alive'. It is acceptable on the screen because we know it as *'playing'*. We seem to forget this fact in our daily lives—the fact that we have created this violent game. It then becomes nearly unstoppable.

It may be why the bombing in Oklahoma City was so interesting or certain celebrity criminal trials so riveting. These and later events—acts of terror—are menacing, but in their own way, are also exhilarating to some people even as they escalate and lead to frustration. And, that's the damned illusion for you.

We've forgotten what is really thrilling. We've forgotten that the Act of Getting Here on Earth in the first place was a far bigger, more exciting adventure.

Patriczia Petrus

So, now, while we are thinking about the possibilities, let's intend to expand on that level of creativity that brought us here in the first place.

With that intention, it is truly possible to transform your current, near-life experience into a real-life adventure without the overwhelming violence. It is time to live the heroic, adventuresome life intended on Earth, not only on the movie & TV screens, but in your space, as well.

Send lite to every fear.

REMINDERS

TRANSFORMING YOUR CURRENT, NEAR-LIFE EXPERIENCE INTO A REAL-LIFE ADVENTURE

It's time to go for the exhilaration without the violence.

When we really see our hand in creation—whether it be bold adventure we wished for or the tiniest direct response to our desire, *it's thrilling*.

The rush is so great because of your *direct involvement*—even with the smallest result.

Here are some examples: you notice a dull relationship spark up or a rocky one smooth out after sending light; you see a very ill child go in the direction of health after sending lite; you notice a personal pain transform to a feeling of bliss after sending light or a frightening weather front pass safely (after sending light to only the picture on The Weather Channel); or long-standing feelings of jealousy, anger, etc., actually soften.

This is the start of turning the near-life experience into a real-life adventure.

So call the Light; summon Joy and transform your heart.

The transformation of the bewildered world follows.

THE PRACTICE

THE OFFER, say,

"I OFFER TO THE DIVINE THIS HAPPY, BLISSFUL, JOYFUL MOMENT (OR EVENT OR FEELING) I AM NOW HAVING."

Also, offer up the *memory* of a joyful, happy, blissful event from the past whenever it may come to mind.

Then, continue to do The Practice.

Send light to every feeling of fear as it arises.

Just say it: "I send lite to this fear."

At the same time, direct the light to where you may feel the negativity in the body:

      – your gut
      – stomach
      – chest
      – throat [7].

Hold your hand (or not) lightly over the area of the body and simply say, "I send light to this feeling," as you feel it rising.

Send lite to every fear. Send lite to every emotion rising.

---

[7] Much is said about directing light to the throat charka in *Talking with Angels*. This is what to do when an overwhelming feeling arises, one that would ordinarily result in tears. Instead, as the feeling moves upward in the body, send the light to the throat. Spill those tears and you could miss an opportunity to *increase your light* and feel even better.

REMINDERS

Avoid reasoning it out:

*"Reason stops breathlessly
        where faith begins.*

*Reason can never reach Heaven
        because it is of the Earth."*

—*Talking with Angels*

*"Make no comparison.
Make no judgments.
Delete your need to understand."*

—W. Brugh Joy, M.D.

During the course of one day, stay out of judgment about what occurs.

At any moment it is possible to remove the mistake of the intellect.

That's progress.

REMINDERS

From the Sufi tradition

If we can live without conditioned reactions for even ten minutes, we are illumined.

Conditioning is the world as we behold it in the narrow, day-to-day way with all of its problems. Light re-conditions and helps to expand one's vision, one's perception—until we truly reach the point of seeing the Unity in it All.

Sometimes that knowing is going to be truly palpable when you see and know each and everything in your environment as yourself and as God. This is a knowing outside of the mind and the ego. This cannot be faked.

Now there are times when the Mind with its fine memory becomes truly useful. It can remind us of that more palpable experience of It All until we are able to sustain it permanently.

So express gratitude to the Mind.

"Simply know that you can slow into the logical mind at any time you really need to—crossing busy intersections, filling out a form at the DMV, doing homework with your second-grader—and eventually you will have a clear knowing of the light guiding even as you do this."

THE PRACTICE

HERE'S A SECRET:

Avoid getting too involved with the questions of the Mind.

It slows you down. Simply, know that *you can slow into the logical mind* at any time you really need to.

No need to concentrate too hard, either.

Once you invite the Light, gently get your mind and ego out of the way.

SIMPLY ALLOW THE DIVINE LIGHT TO DO THE WORK.

Your job is to Call the Light and to Direct the Light.

THEN THE ANGELS TAKE OVER.

SEND LITE TO EVERY FEAR.

REMINDERS

"In the Beginning
God made Creation.
Then, some fools tried to explain it"

—Source unknown

I may be guilty of this kind of explaining. Send lite to the guilty feeling.

From *The Illuminati Papers* of Robert Anton Wilson:

If the world SEEMS TO BE GETTING *B I G G E R and f u n n i e r* all the time, your intelligence is steadily increasing.

If the world seems to be getting *smaller&nastier* all the time, your stupidity is steadily increasing.

Simply Enjoy.

Don't analyze too much.

THE PRACTICE

DEMANDS OF THE MIND

Every time the mind demands an explanation, send lite to the demand.

You know how to say it by now:

> "I send light to the demand" (perhaps directing your hand toward the head).

Eventually the demands and the busy, 'whirring' mind relax and become a more accepting, co-operative partner. Be patient.

After all, the mind is an ally in this practice and is actually performing more creatively than ever before.

Sooner or later the mind will get the message and enjoy its new heightened status.

Neurophysiologist, Sir John Eccles, has been quoted as saying that "We as experiencing persons do not slavishly accept all that is provided for us by our instrument, the neuronal machine of our sensory system and the brain, we select from all that is given according to interest and attention and we modify the actions of the brain, through 'the self' for example, *by initiating some willed movement.*"[8]

SEND LITE TO EVERY FEAR. The ultimate act of will.

8 Sam Parnia, M.D., Ph.D., *What Happens When We Die* (Carlsbad, CA: Hay House, 2006), p.124. Also see "The Self and Its Brain", Routledge, 2003, with K. Popper, for more from Sir John Eccles.

REMINDERS

If you've ever wondered if God has a sense of humor and would like to hear the Creator laugh, simply tell Him your plans.

This also may be another Southern thing; however, it is a good example of how the Mind and the Ego like to work. *It is the Mind and the Ego that are fond of plans and planning.*

O.K., I accept that.

Next, send lite to the plans and turn them over to the Universe for their ideal manifestation.

Each time you do this and directly experience the results, you become more flexible and open to even more possibilities.

"Any individual aligning with the Divine Intent, which is Love, will be at the right place at the right time. He can literally be careless of his whereabouts."

—Peter Erbe

THE PRACTICE

THE EGO

Send lite to the ego's need to control

Just say it:

"I send lite to the ego's need to control."

But, But...send lite to the "buts".

Remember, the weaker the Ego, the more it wants to be in charge.

As the Ego, the 'I' grows stronger as you call Light; it then consciously begins to know itself, too, to be Light, strategically situated right there at the edge of the physical plane through which Spirit expresses.

Ego is a kind of goalie, and it is important to have a strong one on your side. Applaud it. Just keep it in its place so that Pure Intelligence can operate. At some point the two will actually begin to function alike.

PART TWO

ITENSIFYING THE PRACTICE AND BECOMING A *LIGHTWHISPER*:

Ah! To at once Be the Sweetness and Taste the Sweetness. That is the Earth Experience.

Light is the vehicle for love; love sustains us.

EXPANDING YOUR OWN LIGHT:
Light-Matter

As each transformation takes place, your eyes, face and body actually become more radiant.

You radiate more light. *Your halo starts to show—or maybe not.*

You are able to see a new person forming in the mirror as you become Light-Matter.

Then, ask for even more Light and send it to others through your eyes, your hands, your voice, your heart.[9]

Say, "I send light through

> My eyes
> My hands
> My voice
> My heart
> My laughter

To everyone I see, touch or speak to."

Be easy in this practice. Even nonchalant (especially nonchalant). No need to strain or act out of the ordinary. Just be natural. Simply—and consciously—ask that this be the case.

---

9 I have found Sanaya Roman's, *Spiritual Growth* (Tiburon, CA: H. J. Kramer Inc., 1989) to be an especially readable contemporary book on using light. Some language in this practice may reflect that work, which I recommend.

SENDING LIGHT TO OTHERS:

Don't "dis'em", bliss 'em

Invite the Light as you know how.

Then, say:

> "I send Light through my eyes to everyone I look at today."
>
> "I send Light through my hands."
>
> "I send Light through my voice and through my laughter."

Now, get on with your practical life: family, friendships, work, and play.

When, again later, you remember your new 'light-ability', ask again for light and send light.

As another negative emotion arises, send lite to it.

Invoke the Pillar of Light, the Divine Light, the Light of the Supreme Creative Force and direct it to the anxiety or concern. It is done.

When the anxiety is transformed; that is, when you are once again feeling some form or happiness or balance, say "Thanks".

That specific anxiety is now gone forever—or more precisely—is re-shaped into palpable bliss, walking around as you!

SEND LITE TO EVERY FEAR.

ATTENDING TO PHYSICAL PAIN:
A need to be noticed

Do the same thing.

Invite the Light.

Send Light to the location of the pain.[10]

Then, lightly, direct your hand to the pain, holding it over the area (or not). It is important in this practice to stretch your mind somewhat and still do whatever feels natural for you.

The important thing here is to recognize the pain as soon as possible and put attention on it—put light on it. Pain needs to be noticed and attended to.

Then, follow what guidance comes, such as, see a professional; get some rest; continue to send light. Let the pain know you know it is there. It is a part of your self, after all—the part that needs attention now. If you refuse to notice, it may intensify until it gets your attention. Be simple about this; just be immediate.

SEND LITE TO EVERY FEAR.

10 Helena Olsen of Los Angeles, one of the first teachers of Transcendental Meditation in the U.S., taught me both TM® and about directing attention to the body.

Patriczia Petrus

THE WISDOM OF PAIN:

A necessary explanation

At the start of a pain, its cause is often evident and it can be dealt with immediately. However, that is where so many of us humans are in the dark. We miss the early announcement. We are not aware of ourselves and the messages contained therein.

For instance, often a physical problem results from performing some *repetitive actions*—using a part of the body over and over in a way that stresses it. Carpal tunnel, for instance, is an example. The pain is a sign to do something differently or less frequently. Yet, many people miss the first subtle signals.

Whenever you do notice, however, send light to the pain. If it is carpal tunnel, take some vitamin B6 in addition to vitamin B complex. Follow any other prompts to act as well, such as, to see a trusted physician; and continue to use light.

These prompts are forms of light. The more you ask for light, the more information you will spontaneously gather. And as you continue to live with the light—even if you may believe it's only mental—your perception of pain will improve. *Pain can then be addressed and transformed early on, once given the recognition it needs.* Remember, the discomfort is trying to tell you something.

Pain is a wake up call to knowing that *Everything is One.* When that realization truly occurs, the pain morphs into blissful knowing and recognition of it All. *That is the wisdom of pain.*

You can whisper light anywhere—on a bus or plane. No one else needs to know. It's between you and 'you'—that other 'you' being 'whatever you call the source of it All'.

Live in the world as if only you and God lived here.

SEND LITE TO EVERY PAIN.

For instance, rub some essential oil of peppermint on your temples to relieve head tension. As you use light more, you may only need to think of the remedy for it to work, or simply direct the light, or regain the memory of your divine Self in order for the pain to dissipate and be transformed.

SMOOTHING OUT THE MENTAL STUFF:
Transforming unwanted thoughts and doubts

Do the same practice.

Invite the Light.

Send the Light instantly to:

♦ Distressing thoughts
♦ Disappointment
♦ Doubt
♦ Resistance.

Then, relax. It is done.

You have performed the highest act of creative will by inviting the light. It is not necessary to know logically how it works in order for it to work. Your experience will be that it works. Persist somewhat. *Yet, do not be persistent.*

The Supreme Creative Force works out the details once you extend the invitation. Just do the inviting and delete your need to understand, as well.

At first the conditioned mind and the ego may be obstacles and provide resistance; then they become instruments.

ABOUT KEEPING A NOTE PAD:

Evidence for the mind

Do it. It is evidence of progress for the mind and also helps to smooth out and clarify those impudent thoughts, especially.

For starters, use a thick square notepad—the kind that allows you to easily tear off the top page and toss it after it has served its purpose.

Some people get involved with journals which can be very useful, eventually. However, at first, a journal can be more cumbersome and may actually slow this practice.

Ideally, write short notes daily—notes about what concerns you. Keep the process fluid for now as the first transformations occur.

Daily, write down concerns of the mind, anything that needs easing or transforming or enhancing:

- ♦ Little stuff
- ♦ Stupid stuff
- ♦ Big stuff
- ♦ Funny stuff
- ♦ Private stuff
- ♦ Dreams.

Keep the notes short. One idea to a page. Keep it by your bed and play with it before you go to sleep. It seems best to do this at a relaxed time—such as bed time—therefore using a pencil and pad seems more conducive than even something electronic if you are entertaining that.

Regarding your personal concerns and dreams:

"If it's important to you, it's important."

—Rev. Nancy Anderson

THE POINT TO KEEPING NOTES IS:

To send light and to note daily changes

Each day, look at what you wrote the previous day and then note the changes. For example, one day you may have written something like: '*Disturbing interaction with co-worker today*'; or '*embarrassed by getting drinking straw in my nose at lunch*'; or '*disturbing news from Baghdad*'. Be specific with the notes, but not about the outcome.

Remember, then, to send light to the concern or annoyance—whether it's of world importance or something personal that just sticks in your craw.

The next day when you look at your notes, recall if there was any change in the situation. Has the situation lightened up in anyway or are you feeling more at ease about it or are you seeing the humor in it. Whatever is appropriate. *Even the slightest progress is progress*. That is what we build on. Call the *Angels of Build* if you like.

Then, *make a note of the progress*. Throw away the original note if you like.

When noting a situation, keep the following in mind:

♦ We send light to harmonize a situation and not to compel a certain response. Leave that to the Author of It All.

- We express gratitude for each improvement.
- We offer up success.

Eventually discard the notepad, or at least put it away. Start a new one.

This process helps you to see changes that you initiate without continually reviewing the problems as you might in a journal. It keeps you more in the present. It is powerful and practical.

And when writing down your dreams, make them ever more beautiful. Then, start the journal or write the book.

FIRST ALLOW YOURSELF TO ALLOW:
RELATIONSHIPS, SUCCESS, MONEY

A great modern day Vedic astrologer, Pundit Tripathi from India, looked at my *jyotish chart* (astrological chart) and said: "You will have good materialistic comforts, but sometime *you may feel* you are away from them."

I am not asking that you accept astrology of any kind; I am asking that you consider that one's mind and feelings are capable of causing a sense of separation from what is really there.

Sometimes I do allow my mind to separate me from all that is there to nourish me—home, mother, father, children, love, brothers, sisters, and kittens, puppies, cake, Shiraz, dietary supplements and muscle builders, if you must. It's your dream, too.

Allowing everything in life—or not allowing—begins with the mind; then we need to move the mind aside. This is an act of will. So, continuing on with this journey, I ask you to *allow*. Begin by being open to the possibility that everything you could ever want or need is *there already* even if you cannot see it. Even if you are feeling deprived—especially if you are feeling deprived. Send light to this feeling and allow for the good that comes with the transformation of that feeling. Having everything is *all in the allowing*.

Patriczia Petrus

You are beginning to take notice. You send light. You thank each person, pet and thing for existing. Then the senses come into play. You begin to hear, see, feel, taste and smell everything that is already around you; and you are grateful. Everyone and everything is happier. The deer in the yard begin to dance—for you; and the gecko in her habitat catches a cricket and looks at you for approval.

You are now beginning to open the door to it All. Be easy about this and mostly be *compassionate* with yourself and others as well until you have a clear knowing. Remember, when this knowing occurs, it's a *blinding flash of the obvious.*

Ask the intellect and ego to get on board with this knowing. Those were the instruments which guided you here in the first place. Now they need to allow the fulfillment of their work. Continue to give recognition to each gift: i.e., *praise, utilize, and thank each and every thing.* This is a way of giving back to the Author of it All. Then, continue to send light once again to everything and everyone.

This allows more and more beautiful gifts in return.

A BLINDING FLASH OF THE OBVIOUS:

A personal account about the comforts of home

I was having a *black & white* dream in which I lived in a rather ordinary, multi-story house—somewhat like the actual Pennsylvania house in which I grew up.

In the dream, I opened a door leading to the uppermost story and viewed—now *in full color*—a never-before-seen, magnificent dwelling of connecting rooms filled with luxurious furniture upholstered in golden and jeweled-toned fabrics. My heart was full. *"I know this home and have been missing it,"* I realized while still dreaming.

When I awoke, I remembered the dream and felt it must be a memory of a recent *past life*—though I wasn't used to having such memories or even interested in having them. And, since not even Frasier or Niles was available for a dream consultation, I left it at that.

Sometime later, my son and daughter-in-law bought a handsomely restored, Victorian home in Portland, Oregon. It has three main stories, with a truly lavish upper level containing yet two smaller stories (you know the kind which exit out to little porticos). The house even faces due East, a desirable feature in Vedic architecture. Anyway, the first time I actually opened the door to the uppermost level, I recalled the dream. *Now I was certain* the dream was predictive of this house—and it was not the past life memory I had concluded at first.

That was until two years later—when I had the experience of *It All*, the gift of the Light.

This experience did not occur in the upper story of the Portland house. It could have occurred there. *It could have occurred anywhere*; it could have occurred in the street because the experience is the one of knowing that *I am All That; All That is Love; and it is All here to nourish and sustain me.*

At that moment, I realized that I was *facing off with my Self.* Everything in my actual surroundings acquired new and brilliant meaning—like the rooms in the dream. *I was, in fact, in the rooms in the dream and had always been.*

What led up to that moment of knowing is attached to an uncomfortable, recurring emotion having to do with 'houses' and 'neighbors'. I had been sending light to the feelings for several months/years. Now, once more, I was using light to dissolve the same recurring emotion in my gut. At the time, on the shelf stereo in my kitchen, Miriam Makeba was singing, *"Cause We Live for Love."* This time, however, as the feeling in my stomach began to dissolve, *the grand experience of knowing took its place.*

I was/am filled with gratitude for each thing in my presence.

No more mistake of the intellect; no more being separated from the comforts of home. And if I ever think so, I still have my Mind to remind me or I can always recover the knowing in the silence of meditation.

MORE SUCCESS:

It's there ready to be magnified

"I now allow more good things into my life."

—Orin [11]

Each time you allow light, you are allowing God, *if you will*, to communicate with you.

Then, send lite to doubts about **career success.**

Just say it:

"I send light to the seeming visible and invisible obstacle between me and my success."

"I send light to doubts about ever enjoying success."

Light transforms obstacles. "Doubt" is an obstacle. If you are aware of a specific obstacle, send lite to that. See it dissolve.

You are already successful because you are here. Getting a human body is a tremendous accomplishment and comes with a great challenge. You did it. You have the opportunity of knowing God from a brand new POV, point of view. *Send mental postcards Home to the Creator.*

Now allow for the signs and follow the prompts. Have clear intentions. Stay rested. Stay focused. Keep the light strong—like a laser. Everything is for something. Keep on knowing that and appreciate all that is around you.

11 Sanaya Roman, *Spiritual Growth* (Tiburon, CA: H. J. Kramer, Inc., 1989), p.100.

MONEY:

More phoning; less moaning

Call up for some light; lines open 24/7:

*I beckon the light; I become the light: I send lite to obstacles about deserving and magnetizing a personal supply of **money**.*

Say:

"I send light to *doubts* about being deserving and about my ability to magnetize a personal flow of money." And if it is your belief that 'not having' is karmic, send light to the karma and carry on in a way that avoids future negative build up. It's called 'ethics'.

Then, say, *"Thank you for plentiful income."*

Say it often. "Thank you for plentiful income." Write it on your notepad in the evening and allow the manifesting; allow your self to see the possibilities. In the summertime, children see the possibility in lemons when they sell lemonade.

Very important here to follow the prompts when intending to create success and money. You may be presented with a new job, idea, or environment. Or you may choose to bloom where you are planted. If so, send light and transform your concerns about work and work relationships.

Patriczia Petrus

Definitely use the notepad before sleep; and do a review again the next evening. Note any changes—subtle or bold.

It is important to remember that light transforms the obstacles and doubts, establishing both the vehicle and the super highway for fulfillment. Enjoy the ride.

'ETHICS' + 'CONSUMERISM' = ETHICAL CONSUMERISM

The Presence of Infinite Supply

This is a planet which requires the practice of consumerism. Light restores a more *ethical consumerism*. It's about recognizing our values and valuables and exchanging them with others. It's about recognizing that we are valuable and have valuables in the first place.

It is only when people are unable to know with certainty the ***presence of infinite supply*** that greed enters the picture. This picture needs light.

It is not necessarily about judging what ethical behavior is for other individuals or even what a 'good' business is. It is not about boycotting—which relates to the narrative on the topic found in *Wikipedia*—though this may be a choice.

Having and circulating money affords another experience of Unity. It's about seeing the fullness of the Absolute in every transaction and interaction. Once again it is 'play' of sorts. When you have successful transactions, get back to the Author of It All with your applause. This is 'gratitude'.

Remember Your Pin Number to Infinite Supply

You know how I know that you already know this—about infinite supply? *It's because of how we use the term "financially embarrassed"*. We are self-conscious because there is a knowing at our deepest level that we already have everything and we just cannot remember the pin number to access it. Allow more light and the access code becomes evident. Send lite to feeling financially embarrassed.

Income is one area of life that is often imbalanced and conspicuous; we perceive too little or too much money. A person may be born into poverty and later be bored in wealth—or visa versa. One may have the experience of both extremes and not be satisfied either way because the 'light' part of the equation is missing—the part that is fullness or God. Send lite to feelings of dissatisfaction.

For many, winning the lottery is an example of 'too much too soon'; the intensity is jarring and can be unhealthy.

When something like this happens, *ask for balance* and enjoy. Get some good investment advice along the way.

RELATIONSHIPS:
Important light bytes

It is important to send light and to extend love where there is no obvious return—especially if there is no obvious return.

Send lite to **obstacles** that appear to be blocking harmonious and loving **relationships**.

Say:

> "I send light to act on the obstacles between myself and my heart's mate. I send light to 'doubt' about ever knowing/enjoying this person."

That person is already there in your heart. Now allow their presence and go about your business.

Remember to send light to remove obstacles limiting all relationships: with co-workers, family members, neighbors, those who provide you with services—whoever and whenever you think of these.

You may say:

> "It is my intention to have more harmonious relationships."

Then consider this: "Though there may be seeming obstacles such as finance, geography, status, age and/or health, I accomplish better relationships by first transforming negative feelings about these ideas that I carry within myself. *These negative feelings or feelings of non-acceptance of others within me are in fact obstacles.*"

Send light to the feelings as they show up and where they show up within the body.

Keep the heartlight on.

LOVING OTHER PEOPLE:

ST. TERESA OF AVILA MEETS CRASH OF HOLLYWOOD

There are records that Teresa of Avila, a saint in the Catholic Church, was filled with a passion—the light of God. Yet she was also known to teach "that the mark of spiritual understanding was not the degree of bliss that a person experienced or how much he or she loved God, *but how much he or she was able to love other people.*"[12]

No one dare say just how another person is to express love. Not all of us are Peace Corp material, missionaries, or saints; yet all are options. Love does start, however, with *recognition* —with the recognition that we are all in this earth experience together. The 2005 Academy Award winning movie, *CRASH*, epitomizes the experience for me. I had seen this film when I was finishing the updates on this book. The theme exemplifies how violent behavior can open the door for light/love. Once we get that, it's important to remember to send light *before* the situation escalates and becomes violent. It takes an act of will.

In a way, interpersonal relationships—and not just the romantic ones—are a final frontier. I am not the first to say that. The challenge is great. And, until you have the real inner knowing of who others are, send light to each sticky situation and respect/enjoy differences in people.

Patriczia Petrus

For example, greater than the fear of death is the fear of public speaking (incidentally, high up there with the fear of snakes). Speaking publicly means facing other people—people you may perceive as different from yourself. Experts have recommended picturing your audience naked or wearing clown suits. People are supposed to appear less threatening—and more vulnerable—when wearing funny clothes or nothing.

Personally, I prefer to see an audience as an outpicturing of myself (wearing funny clothes or nothing, of course). Then send light to each and every one—and to your fearful emotion. It helps to prepare your talk well and look into taking some Kava kava, the socializing herb of Fiji and the South Pacific to put you at ease.

12 Jane Hope, *The Secret Language of the Soul* (London: Duncan Baird Publishers 1997), 225.

RELATIONSHIP OUTCOME:

Be magnanimous about the result

The situation always improves when you choose to send light to someone else.

When you choose to send light to someone, you need to have the intention of allowing that individual to use the light freely as he/she wishes. It needs to be given freely as it was given to you.

When you send light to the other person in a relationship, have the intention that the relationship be harmonized:

> *This could mean the relationship deepens or even disappears.*

Your Higher Self knows.

Remind yourself that "I do not intend to create a specific result—with one exception: that any change brings greater happiness and freedom for all involved." Send lite to all personal concerns, fears, anxieties about a relationship. Send light to concerns around your relationships with your employer or employees; friends; neighbors; relatives.

Patriczia Petrus

And remember to embrace and enjoy the differences in all people. This is recreational in a kindhearted way. *Above all be kind.*

> *Being kind opens the door to becoming harmless.*
>
> *Intending no harm opens the door to It All.*

A LIGHT REVIEW OF LIFE:

A time to transform existing and past relationships

I do this when I'm very relaxed—before sleep, when traveling (not doing the driving), or taking a quiet walk. It's like using the notepad mentally. This time I allow past memories and their accompanying feelings to come up. Then, send light to these memories and emotions. If they are uncomfortable ones, keep sending the light. If the memories are enjoyable ones, offer them to the Author of It All. Now allow for even more enjoyable experiences.

Sending light to past experiences harmonizes relationships with those individuals *in the present time*. Light gets rid of old baggage; it's the baggage handler.

You may start by sending love and light to an existing relationship. Say:

I invoke the light. I become the light. I send the loving light to my relationship

   …with my daughter (by name).

   …with my son (by name).

This keeps a beautiful relationship growing and creates harmonious new relationships.

Send light to someone who has died. Say:

> I send loving light to my relationship with my mother
> (by name and who died in 1983).

Yes, you can harmonize a relationship with someone who has passed away and actually experience a difference today—in your heart and mind as well. Remember, *PastPresentFuture*, All One. Send light to the relationship or to an event in the past.

If you doubt that, then start by sending love and light to the 'doubt'. Intend to transform the doubt, then move on to the relationship.

You are able to do a review of your life consciously and make a difference using light. Just be easy.

At other times, remember to keep sending light to any uncomfortable emotions that arise spontaneously.

Send lite to every fear.

SICK OF SENDING LIGHT?

When your get sick of sending light, send light to the sick feeling and forget it.

This can happen and does. Then, it's time to just forget about it and go about your activities. Don't be concerned about anything.

Later, you will remember that you have this new tool and be happy again.

It is important to remind others that *there is something that can be done* anywhere and anytime. You might want to have some personal experience first.

Also, it is important to have a friend in this light experiment to remind you when some shadow covers you up. Just like it's important to have a friend when you are physically sick to remind you to have some soup or to take the olive leaf extract to fight a virus; or to take some valerian root extract to help you sleep. I notice that even the person most knowledgeable about herbs and natural medicines sometimes forgets what to use when an illness takes over.

When you get sick of anything, even yourself, call the light and follow the prompts. Go outside; enjoy the sun and wind and sounds of nature. Go to a movie. It may have new meaning.

Patriczia Petrus

EVENTS—REAL, IMAGINARY, DREAMED, TELEVISED

There is no such thing as "just imagination".
There are only realities that have not been
magnetized to you yet.

Once you become a carrier of light and you see that it is really working (check your daily notes for affirmation), then it is important to realize that your thoughts and desires are growing more powerful. Remember to:

♦ Offer up the beautiful one.

♦ Send light to the weird, stressful ones to be transformed into harmonious representations.

♦ Send light to an event occurring today, tomorrow, at home, in another state, yesterday, last month, 25 years ago. (In my experience it has taken about 20 minutes for light to reach Iowa, for instance, from North Carolina, really.)

♦ Simply invoke light and send it to a memory or the thought of a future event as it comes to mind. It does not matter where it is.

As I was updating this information on a Saturday morning, August 5, 2006, National Public Radio's Car Talk experts were conversing with a priest, Father John (from Portland, Oregon). Father John said that whenever his older model car broke down, he would lay his hands on it and 30 seconds later it would start up. The hosts suggested the priest could make a lot of money with that talent though they did not explain the phenomenon mechanically.

Here's what I am getting at, you can call the light every day—and *when there is nothing left to do*. Couldn't hurt.

TV & MOVIES: REEL OR REAL?

A new level of personal accountability—
while eating popcorn

This point can make your viewing time more worthwhile and interesting.

You are able to send light to a negative event you are watching in a theatre, on a DVD, or on television. The scene may be either actual or fictional. Consciously you may direct light to the vision through your eyes or with your hand, or through the heart. These scenes are no less your Self, your creation, than anything else in your life.

Under any circumstances what you take in with your senses is all "food". What you choose to listen to, to view, to smell, to touch and of course to taste—it's all metabolized by your mind and body. Now, consider adding a new level to the viewing—that of *consciously sending light to what you view or hear in order to effect a harmonious change.* Metabolize light along with everything else.

For example when/if you choose to watch Oprah or the news or a film with a violent twist or even a storm on The Weather Channel, you may intend that the difficulty you are observing be resolved for everyone, everywhere, who is going through the same kind of situation.

If, however, you are watching a truly wondrous scene, then have the intention of offering it up.

TRANSFORM IT FOR YOU AND FOR THE WORLD:

A personal event

The date had to be April 3, 1996. As I woke up that morning in Thousand Oaks, California, I did not really pay attention to the calendar. I was on vacation from North Carolina and except for the fact that I needed to be aware enough of the day and time to board the Amtrak, I was enjoying a beautiful California spring morning with my family.

This day my itinerary included a train trip to north San Diego County to visit friends. The train was leaving Ventura County, California, for Union Station in Los Angeles; and from there would continue to San Diego. I took my entire luggage with me because in a day or two, I was going to fly directly back to North Carolina.

The train ride was fascinating—with one 'gentleman' strolling the aisle commenting on how Amtrak consumes government funds (in much more colorful language than that). My seat mate was an older lady traveling only as far as Anaheim, California, to visit with her "extraordinary" daughter. Her family was all connected to the medical field: and there was a great deal of self-absorption with the topic, I recall. Yet, it was somewhat entertaining to listen and observe. After all, it was a beautiful day and *I do believe that up to that point, Amtrak was on time.*

We arrived in Los Angeles' Union Station and the scene changed. After an unusually long wait on board in the station, an announcement was made to the passengers on my train. We were told to gather our baggage and depart the train. Passengers were being transferred to a bus and driven to San Diego and points south. The specific reason given was that *"there is a bomb on the 4th Street overpass"* which was en route.

Everyone disembarked, speedily and nervously except for me. I waited in my seat. I needed to ask an attendant for assistance with my extra luggage. I was told someone would come. I waited and waited. No one came. I got off the train and looked down the track. This huge boarding area was empty and silent. I was alone.

That is when I remembered the *Light*. Standing next to the track, I began to direct my hand in the direction of the 4th Street overpass. I said something like *"I send Light to the 4th Street overpass."* I did this for more than 10 minutes. I felt okay—even calm. If I missed the Amtrak bus, I knew I would get to San Diego somehow. More than 30 minutes had passed since the other passengers departed.

After several more minutes, I heard distant voices breaking through the silence. There were a lot of voices and gradually they grew louder and more distinguishable. The sound was coming from the tunnel that led to the busses. *The passengers from my train were returning.*

After everyone stored luggage and once again took seats, I learned that the situation with the bomb on 4th Street had passed, and safely so. (At the time, no one could offer a complete explanation. *I would look for it on the news that evening,* I thought.)

I was once more seated next to my original seat mate. She was very different now. She seemed vulnerable and no longer so self-assured. I took her hand and said little.

Later that evening, I was sitting on the sofa bed in the living room of my friend's San Diego apartment and remembered it was time for the news. There was nothing about the 4th Street incident in Los Angeles. The big news, however, was that *the Unabomber was captured that day.*

For the sake of clarification, the Unabomber, who for nearly 18 years created terror in the United States with mail bombs, was in Montana not Los Angeles. Were these two incidents —the train bomb and the Unabomber capture—connected physically and practically? No. Were they connected on some other level? This is what we are coming to realize: how far-reaching light is and the Oneness of it All.

I am making no claims, after all there seems to have been a great deal of planning that led up to the Unabomber's capture. Many will call this coincidental. But what is a coincidence? I am just presenting the facts, ma'am, from my perspective on that train track. I sent light with the intention of clearing the overpass and more than one bomb-related problem resolved the same day.

Send lite to every fearful situation. Transform it for you; and you may just be transforming it for the world.

[I committed this incident to writing for the first time on August 9, 2006. After intensely focusing on and reliving these events for several hours, I finished writing at 4:15 p.m., Pacific Time. The following day there was the news that British security officials had thwarted a group which was planning to use liquids to create explosives on British flights to the

U.S. The apprehension took place just as I had finished writing this which was just after midnight, London time. Was this connected? Reportedly many months of planning also went into the London capture yet the event occurred simultaneously with this project. And, though I had verbally told the original Los Angeles story from time to time, I had never put very much attention and light on it until this writing on August 9, 2006.

I wish to be clear that I am not claiming any special talents—talents that are not already inherent in every human being. I am saying the world is as large or as small as we make it, literally.]

THE WISDOM OF ANGER, VIOLENCE AND EVEN WAR:

Conditions of 'extreme enlightenment' reveal our true nature

Does everyone but me have this wisdom already? If so, you may skip ahead. The reason I ask is because in TV sitcoms couples get angry all the time and argue just so they can make up. So anger gets them back to *love*—or to something like love. Let's extrapolate this premise and take a look at more extreme, though similar, situations.

For example, I recently watched on DVD a film originally made for the BBC entitled *Love in a Cold Climate*.[13] The time was 1940-41 and a disparate English family is driven back to their childhood country estate by the threat of bombs falling in Paris and London. Even family members, not seen for a decade, are returning. The clouds of war are gathering—and so are families. The war and bombs are bringing them home again. The family is finding love again. Is this, then, the beauty of the bomb and the wisdom of war? The method seems extremely destructive, *but at the same time it's equally unifying.*

13 BBC Production ©2000 BBC Masterpiece Theatre of Nancy Mitford's novels *The Pursuit of Love* and *Love in a Cold Climate*.

Again, I ask, *can we go for the unity without the violence?* Or could it be that when you and I and the Creator were preparing this grand design called Earth, we wrote in the bombs as *cues* or *prompts* to get us to reunite—as a way back to our oneness. (Likewise for *déjà vu* experiences, these are customarily construed as an illusion of something that occurred previously. Instead, could a déjà vu experience be a *faint reminder* or a marker of our grand designs for this lifetime, cueing us that we are on the right track?)

Back on point, in 2006 as we witness increased violence in the Middle East, at the same time we see peace groups coming together all over the world to meditate or to pray. Individuals are uniting with common purpose; and there is love and bliss in this togetherness. War is bringing the troops of peace together. More light and love is emanating as the bombs get noticed.

This violence is being recognized—perhaps not consciously yet—as an aspect of the Self, something of our own creation. As we attend to it, it gets transformed. Granted the bombings make a loud noise to get our attention—however, not unlike a parent who has to call very loudly when the child or puppy starts to wander off. In a way the bombs are speaking for God, or our Higher Self, saying *"I am so angry that you do not recognize Me that I am going to cry out or make a really big noise to get your attention."* It is done to regain recognition and acceptance. A big fuss gets noticed.

And about antagonism of any kind, remember that the best revenge is *to know everything as your Self* whether it's a rambunctious child or a destructive bomb.

"I am the Universe." Knowing this makes each of us ultimately accountable—and kind.

LOVE & WAR IN FOREIGN LANDS:

Bomblets of wisdom

Families gain new appreciation of each other as individual members get called away to foreign lands. This, too, brings up the question "Are there really 'foreign lands'?" Or, is this calling away just more of a trip of re-discovery intended by our Higher Self from the beginning of our Earth adventure.

This front page story headlined **Joined by love and war**[14] from *The Oregonian* newspaper, Sunday, July 23, 2006, could have been told in *The Des Moines Register* or *The Sacramento Bee* or in any paper, *any where in the world*.

The Oregonian story carried the subtitle *"An Oregon National Guardsman and his Iraqi bride find happiness in America after braving terror threats and the deadly streets of Baghdad."*

Before going further, I keep thinking that *it's all about the kiss;* it's all about love and about getting back *home*. As Earth adventurers, we go through all kinds of trials to get to the love—both in real life and *in reel life,* the movies. Think about it? (Or, review the top 50 adventure movies of all time, on line.)

According to the newspaper story, **Joined by love and war**, 27 months after they met, on the day they were getting married, the American groom asked the Iraqi bride-to-be,

"Why are you marrying me.?"

"My heart is stupid," she is quoted, *"I love you."*

A very true and simple response after months of war and obstacles. The heart is foolish and that simply means that the heart is unobstructed; the heart is without conditions; the heart is nourished by love.

So again here is the wisdom of war, the beauty of it. Historically, destruction has *prompted* love and life; I'm talking about you, *baby boomers*, an extraordinary result of 'war and love'. Now how can we get to the love without the destruction? Or do we really want to? Is there a less violent way for the hero and heroine to kiss in the end and discover their oneness? Or, for families and groups to reconnect—to recognize that we are all in this great adventure together?

Call Light. Send Light until we are able to recognize the good in all things—until our eyes are wide open to our true nature, to the extraordinary brilliance of our world and the comforts of home which are manifesting all around us as we *relax in our forever omnipresence*.

14 Julie Sullivan, "Joined by love and war," *The Oregonian*, 23 July, 2006, sec. 1A, p.1.

ARE YOU HAVING FUN YET?

Are you remembering to take your vitamins and omega 3's? Are you remembering to get enough sleep and to meditate, to walk outside and to look at the sky, to breathe? Are you remembering your power to create yet?

Be patient and courageous. You will.

The purpose of creation is the expansion of happiness, the Vedas tell us.

When you regain the memory of your ability *to create, you will have also greater and greater experiences of happiness.*

Your body is the system through which this creation is getting back on track and finally being fulfilled. You are a *transducer* for the power source. The purpose of your nervous system is to convert Divine Light to be usable on Earth. Each person has this ability to Call Light and Become Light. The ability grows the more it is used.

The response likewise grows more evident. Also, the *responsibility* becomes greater *and grows lighter at the same time.* You become happier and may even feel shallow—less troubled. As you grow more powerful, you become less full of yourself—that old, heavy self.

"God is present on earth because you are."

—Ken Carey

It is your choice to Invite the Light and fulfill your Purpose. This is the great act of will.

SEND LITE TO EVERY FEAR

NO STRINGS ATTACHED;

NO PUPPETS IN SIGHT

If you did not have the choice to invite the light, you would be a puppet.

You are, however, an individualized living being with the ability to grow more radiant every moment by electing to transform the shadows and consciously choosing to heavenize this planet. Your body contains the seeds to grow heaven on earth—*Thy Will be done in earth as it is in Heaven.* The question has always been *how?* The answer has always been *light*—there in plain sight.

I am not the first to realize that there is more to being on earth then to be danced around, puppet-like, and then sent back to the prop room or at best, to central casting like an extra player. Shakespeare espoused *"all the world's a stage."* Earth is venue for our creativity not puppetry.

It is a brand, new venue in creative terms. Earth is an adventure in Light and Dark, Spirit and Body/Matter. And, only with a precious physical body is that even possible. Don't throw it away. It is truly a living temple waiting to be flooded with Light.

Invite the Light at any age—8, 18, or 80.

"Thus this magnificent civilization...goes happily and joyfully on forever. For, of course, anything will want to go on forever when it is fully assured of its beauty...and its beauty ever increasing."[15]

Therefore, dream ever more beautifully for an ever more beautiful, enlivened and fascinating reality.

15 J.F. Lynch, San Diego, CA, in a personal message

GRATITUDE

The Creator responds, "I'll see you and raise you."

Be grateful for this life. Be grateful for music. Be grateful for friends. Be grateful for It All. In other words, recognize the good around you all of the time. The Creator will then match that good and raise you.

When you have any experience of joy or feeling happy—no matter how tiny an increase—express gratitude.

At first, new feelings may come in baby steps. Watch for them. Trust them and send light to any doubts about your participation in the creation of these new feelings.

The more you recognize and appreciate, the more you spontaneously honor and express gratitude; then, the more you allow for good things to come to you. So say 'thanks'—it can be silent—for the smallest improvement and also *be sure to acknowledge your hand in its creation.*

Keep on keeping the notepad until you are recognizing the differences moment to moment. Eventually gratitude will be implied through your pure enjoyment of it all—no words or thoughts required. You are, then, simply enfolded in All That Is.

Send lite to every fear *and put joy in its place.*

Out creator would never have made such lovely days and
have given us the deep hearts to enjoy them unless we were
meant to be immortal.

—*Nathanial Hawthorne*

PART THREE

CONSCIOUS IMMORTALITY

About Death and the Seamless Transition

"To get a human body is a rare thing...make full use of it... After getting a human body, if you don't reach God, then you have sold a diamond at the price of spinach."

—Swami Brahmananda Saraswati

From the finite to the infinite, at last:

Some reminders

"Life does not die because it gets worn out.
It dies because it has not found itself."

—Sri Aurobindo[16]

We are looking for life in all the wrong places; it is, after all, hidden in plain sight.

A great master, Sri Aurobindo, speaks of these near-life experiences we've been entertaining. It seems that even ordinary yogic consciousness only suffices to prolong life, create immunity from disease and supply youthfulness. What we are seeking is "to transform life, not plaster the façade."

It is not a matter of passing on to a better existence in order to enjoy more good, but a matter of transforming the present existence. After all, it is all One—a continuum. At the very least, it's possible *to begin* now and therefore, allow for the possibility of more seamless transitions.

Send lite to every fear. Send lite to every doubt.

16 Today is August 15, 2006: and I discovered as I began the review of this page that it is Sri Aurobindo birthday. What are the chances I would be doing the update of this page on this day? In the world that I am now allowing, there could be no other way. It is a marker. It is all One. It is all Now.

About reincarnation:

Is it really better in Hawaii?

"I've been alive forever, and I wrote the very first song," writes The Beach Boys' Bruce Johnston in this insightful song lyric. He was speaking of *Music*.

Like music, we've all been around forever. Let's say we've had other bodies, other lives, maybe even in Kauai or some other Eden-like setting. Have we grown in awareness throughout these incarnations? Or, have we experienced centuries— rather than only decades—of stagnancy with its mixed results of pain and frustration and some happiness.

In the late 1880's, psychologist/philosopher William James *"predicted that within 25 years science would resolve once and for all whether the dead could speak to the living."*[17] His confident estimation was based on new knowledge of radio and electromagnetic waves and their projected power.

So I ask you, a quarter of a century later in 1905, had history reported that we were, in a facile way, having this communication? I don't think so. How about by the year 2005? Yet, there is deep knowing in this matter and real value in James' prediction although it has not manifested in the way he indicated—yet.

The purpose of reincarnation, many interpret, is to grow in awareness; yet the Spirit is already Pure Awareness. So then,

"All we have to do is improve our knowing," says Parmahansa Yogananda.

Likewise, artist Mellen-Thomas Benedict stated after a near-death experience[18] that: *"Spirit is not pushing us to dissolve this body."* He says, *"living forever in one body is not as creative as reincarnation"* which he describes as a *"transferring of energy in this fantastic vortex of energy that we are in."* So that after 150 year or so, we may want to *"change channels,"* according to Benedict.

May I suggest, then, that we prepare ourselves to change channels *consciously* in order to begin living a *conscious immortality?* It's just a suggestion; after all, forever omnipresence may be too new (or too old) an idea and takes some getting used to or recalling. At the very least, entertain it for a while and send light to any questions.

17 Patricia Cohen, "Ghost Hunters': Seeking Science in Séance," The New York Times, 14 Aug 2006, Books of the Times.
18 "Mellen-Thomas Benedict's Near-death Experience." *Near Death Experiences and the Afterlife.* http://www.near-death.com/

It is simply not good enough to be immortal if...

if we are not conscious of it.

Through meditation, prayer and intention, we open the space for communication with the Source, with Light. Light improves our memory and reveals our true nature. When we realize this, our job is just then beginning or rather starting up again. It's like awaking from a long siesta. Are we then learning about light and shadow only to continue to bob back and forth forever between great exhilaration and deep frustration? Or, will we choose to embrace the *limited darkness* with our true *light without limits* thereby transforming the shadows forever?

Furthermore, *about death*, feel free to choose number 1, 2, or 3:

1. You may depart, knowing there is not necessarily more awareness after death then you have right now. Remember, it could very well be that *"if you are thick as two planks when you are alive, you are thick as two planks when you are dead,"* suggests Stuart Wilde.

2. You may stay—and continue to forget about the Light and that there is *something you can do everyday and when there is nothing left to do.*

3. You may choose to stay, read some of these pages again and invite the Light, which prepares you for a more

conscious departure later on—say after 150 years or all right after only 120 years.

After all who would not want to go on forever with eyes wide open in a universe of vast possibilities and immense beauty?

Each today, well-lived, makes yesterday a dream of happiness
And tomorrow a vision of all possibilities.
Look, therefore, to this one day, for it alone is life.

—Essence of a Sanskrit poem

IN CONCLUSION:

A new and joyous, defining moment in the history of our planet

A great secret is that Truth *contains* rather than *excludes* all things; it encompasses all—both shadow and light. Invite the light and lovingly embrace the shadows. Endeavor to bring the shadows home into the Light where they are transformed. Then you will truly know your many-faceted self and experience Love as never before. You will know it *All as One* and *All as your Self.*

This is our chance for Heaven and Earth to be *equal and one* and for balance to be restored to a bewildered world. Give Light a chance. Send light to every fear and be prepared to embrace *a new defining moment* in the history of this planet —one you won't have to 'shout to the Heavens' because in that moment, heaven moves right into your neighborhood.

Lastly, do not accept any of this unless it agrees with your own reason and common sense. If what you have read is agreeable, even if for now it seems like fiction, you're invited to join me and all the others in this magnificent adventure. I am looking forward to knowing you—*once more.*

Let us be radiating truth, the light of life.
Never shall we denounce anyone, never entertain negativity.

A Bibliography

This is a short list of books I am happy to have known. Some have provided reminders or suggested language personalized in the practice for *Send Lite to Every Fear*. Others have been purely inspirational.

Aïvanhov, Omraam Mikhaël, *Light is a living spirit.* © Editions Prosveta 1998. Prosveta S.A.-B.P.12-83601 Fréjus CEDEX (France). ISBN 2-85566-391-1.

Carey, Ken, *The Starseed Transmissions and Starseed, The Third Millennium.* © 1991 by Kenneth X. Carey. HarperCollins Publishers, 10 East 53rd Street, New York, NY 10023.

Chopra, M.D., Deepak, *Unconditional Life: mastering the forces that shape personal reality.* © 1991. Bantam Books, New York.

Erbe, Peter, *God, I Am, from Tragic to Magic.* Triad Publishing Pty, Ltd., Australia.

Gibran, Kahlil, *Jesus, the Son of Man.* © 1928 Kahlil Gibran. Source of material from Alfred K. Knoph, Inc., Random House Inc., New York.

Gorbunov, Yuri, *Lectures on Modern Theosophy, Agni Yoga and Tibetan Teaching.* © 2003 Gorbunov & Keane.

Hope, Jane, *The Secret Language of the Soul.* © 1997. Duncan Baird Publishers, London.

I Ching, The Book of Changes. Translated by Frank J. MacHovec. © 1971 by the Peter Pauper Press, Inc., Mt Vernon, NY.

Levacy, William R., *Beneath a Vedic Sky.* © 1999 by William R. Levacy. Hay House, Carlsbad, CA. (a source for information about jyotish)

Parnia, Sam, M.D., Ph.D., *What Happens When We Die* © by 2006 Sam Parnia. Hay House, Carlsbad, CA.

Pope John Paul, *Gift and Mystery.* © 1996. Doubleday, New York.

Mahesh Yogi, Maharishi, *Maharishi Mahesh Yogi on the Bhagavad-gita:* a new translation and commentary with Sanskrit text. © 1969. Harmondsworth, Penguin.

Mallasz, Gitta, *Talking with Angels.* © 1988, 1992 by Daimon Verlag, AM Klosterplatz, CH-8840 Einsiedeln, Switzerland.

Marciniak, Barbara, *Bringers of the Dawn: teachings from the Pleiadians.* © 1992. Bear & Co., Santa Fe, NM.

Roman, Sanaya, *Spiritual Growth.* © 1989 by Sanaya Roman. Published by H.J. Kramer Inc., P. O. Box 10982, Tiburon, CA 94920.

Satprem; translated from the French by Luc Venet. *Sri Aurobindo, or, The adventure of consciousness.* © 1984. Institute for Evolutionary Research, New York.

Spangler, David. *The Laws of Manifestation.* © 1975. Findhorn Foundation, Forres, Scotland.

Thiede, Carsten Peter, *Eyewitness to Jesus : amazing new manuscript evidence about the origin of the Gospels.* Carsten Peter Thiede and Matthew D'Ancona. © 1996. Doubleday, New York.

Tomioka, Ariel, *On the Breath of the Gods*, International ed. [Carmichael, CA: Helios House]; [S.I.] : Pythagorean Press of Australia and New Zealand, © 1990.

Urantia Book, The, © Jan 1955 Urantia Foundation, Chicago. IL. 60614.

Upanishads, The [classic Vedic texts]. Many editions available.

Vivekananda, Swami, *Raja-yoga* (yoga aphorisms of Patanjali). 1937. Frameries, Belgique, Union des imprimeries (s.a.) Dépositaires généraux: Paris, A.Maisonneuve [etc].

Wilde, Stuart, *Affirmations.* © 1987 by Stuart Wilde. Published by Hay House, Carlsbad, CA.

Wilson, Robert Anton, *The Illuminati Papers.* © 1980, 1997 Robert Anton Wilson Published by Ronin Publishing, Inc. P.O. Box 522, Berkeley, CA 94701.

Yogananda, Parmahansa., *Where There is Light: insight and inspiration for meeting life's challenges/selections from the teachings of P. Yogananda.* © 1988 Self-Realization Fellowship, Los Angeles, California.

Talks, Websites:

Anderson, Rev. Nancy, talks at the Church of Religious Science, Encinitas, CA.

Welles, Geoffery PhD., "Mistake of the Intellect", © 1987 *MIU Video Magazine*, Maharishi University of Management, Fairfield, IA.

"Mellen-Thomas Benedict's Near-death Experience." *Near Death Experiences and the Afterlife* © 2005 at http://www.near-death.com/

About the Author

Disguised as a broadcaster in Southern California, and later as a university PR director in Iowa, Patriczia was looking to get through the wall of materiality to the underlying Divine Source. This has been a conscious quest since age 4 when she began questioning mortality at "wakes" in her Northeastern PA birthplace. As a human potential pioneer, she created a wellness column for health care professionals; produced radio shows (KGIL, Los Angeles); and chartered New Awareness courses. Her career has put her in the company of Peter Caddy and David Spangler of Findhorn; Maharishi Mahesh Yogi; Muktananda; leading doctors, ie; Deepak Chopra; visionary Og Mandino; and movie, magic and music luminaries including Eastwood, Henning and Zappa.

She uses language, music and intuition as guides armed with a degree in English and Education from Marywood University, along with studies in Latin, and subsequently, in Sanskrit and Applied Music.

While compiling this litany, Patriczia remained focused and lived simply in the North Carolina mountains near Blowing Rock. While there, she acquired a position as adjunct faculty in Communications at Appalachian State University, a branch of the University of North Carolina. Presently she lives on the central coast of Oregon where she completed the updates for *Send Lite to Every Fear.*